GERMAN CONSTITUTIONAL LAW

Books LLC®, Reference Series, Memphis, USA, 2011. www.booksllc.net. Copyright: http://creativecommons.org/licenses/by-sa/3.0/deed.en

Table of Contents

German constitutional law
Basic Law for the Federal Republic of Germany 1
Federal Constitutional Court of Germany 5
German Federal Constitutional Court abortion decision 7
Herrenchiemsee convention 8
Streitbare Demokratie 8

Judges of the Federal Constitutional Court of Germany
Andreas Voßkuhle 8
Brun-Otto Bryde 9
Christine Hohmann-Dennhardt 9
Erna Scheffler 9
Ernst-Wolfgang Böckenförde 10
Ernst Benda 10
Ernst Träger 11
Evelyn Haas 11
Everhardt Franßen 12
Ferdinand Kirchhof 12
Franz Wessel 12

Gebhard Müller 12
Gertrude Lübbe-Wolff 13
Hans-Jürgen Papier 13
Hans Georg Rupp 14
Hans Hugo Klein 14
Helga Seibert 15
Hermann Höpker-Aschoff 15
Johannes Masing 15
Josef Wintrich 15
Jutta Limbach 15
Jürgen Kühling 16
Karin Graßhof 16
Klaus Winter 16
Konrad Hesse 16
Lerke Osterloh 17
Michael Eichberger 17
Paul Kirchhof 17
Renate Jaeger 18
Roman Herzog 18
Rudolf Katz 19
Rudolf Mellinghoff 20
Susanne Baer 20
Udo Di Fabio 20

Udo Steiner 20
Walter Rudi Wand 21
Willi Geiger (judge) 21
Winfried Hassemer 21
Wolfgang Zeidler 21

Referendums in Germany
East Prussian plebiscite 22
German election and referendum, 1936 25
German election and referendum, 1938 26
German referendum, 1933 26
German referendum, 1934 26
Schleswig Plebiscites 27

State constitutions of Germany
Constitution of Hamburg 28
Constitution of Hesse 29
Constitution of North Rhine-Westphalia 29

Introduction

Purchase of this book entitles you to a free trial membership in the publisher's book club at www.booksllc.net. (Time limited offer.) Simply enter the barcode number from the back cover onto the membership form. The book club entitles you to select from hundreds of thousands of books at no additional charge. You can also download a digital copy of this and related books to read on the go. Simply enter the title or subject onto the search form to find them.

Each chapter in this book ends with a URL to a hyperlinked online version. Type the URL exactly as it appears. If you change the URL's capitalization it won't work. Use the online version to access related pages, websites, footnotes, tables, color photos, updates. Click the version history tab to see the chapter's contributors. Click the edit link to suggest changes.

A large and diverse editor base collaboratively wrote the book, not a single author. After a long process of discussion and debate, the chapters gradually took on a neutral point of view reached through consensus. Additional editors expanded and contributed to chapters striving to achieve balance and comprehensive coverage. This reduced the regional or cultural bias found in many other books and provided access and breadth on subject matter otherwise little documented.

Basic Law for the Federal Republic of Germany

The **Basic Law for the Federal Republic of Germany** (German: *Grundgesetz für die Bundesrepublik Deutschland*) is the constitutional law of Germany. It was formally approved on 8 May 1949, and, with the signature of the Allies, came into effect on 23 May 1949, as the constitution of those states of West Germany that were initially included within the Federal Republic. Within a few years, the Federal Republic included all of West Germany, i.e. those parts of Germany under American, British, or French occupation.

The German word *Grundgesetz* may be translated as either *Basic Law* or **Fundamental Law** (*Grund* is cognate with the English word *ground*). The term *Verfassung* (constitution) was not used, as the drafters regarded the *Grundgesetz* as a provisional constitution for the provisional West German state and would not prejudice the decisions of a future reunified Germany to adopt a constitution. Shortly after its adoption, the East German Soviet occupation zone was transformed into the communist German Democratic Republic (GDR) with its own constitution.

Germany was reunified in 1990 after the Communist regime in East Germany was toppled and the GDR peacefully joined the Federal Republic of Germany. Article 23 of the Basic Law was used in reunification when East Germany, which had been unitary since 1949, re-divided into its original *länder*, with Berlin as a new city-state (like Bremen and Hamburg). After reunification, the Basic Law remained in force, having proved itself as a stable foundation for the thriving democracy in West Germany that had emerged from the ruins of World War II. Some changes were made to the law in 1990, mostly pertaining to reunification, such as to the preamble. Additional major modifications of the Basic Law were made in 1994, 2002 and 2006.

Drafting process

Article 1, sentence 1 ("Human dignity is inviolable.")

> " *We must be sure that what we construct will some day be a good house for all Germans.* "
> — Karl Arnold speaking about the objective of the West German Basic Law at the Koenig Museum, 1948

The idea for the creation of the Basic Law came originally from the three western occupying powers. In view of the Nazi usurpation of Germany's pre-war Weimar Constitution, they made their approval of the creation of a new German state conditional on

- A complete rejection of the ideology that the German people are a master race (German: *Herrenvolk*) superior to others and entitled to commit genocide, or to treat barbarically those not belonging to it;
- An unequivocal commitment to the inviolability and inalienability of human rights.

The draft was prepared at the Herrenchiemsee convention (10 – 23 August 1948) on the Herreninsel in the Chiemsee, a lake in southeastern Bavaria. The delegates at the Convention were appointed by the leaders of the newly formed *Länder* (states). After being passed by the Parliamentary Council assembled at the Museum Koenig in Bonn on 8 May 1949 — the Museum was the only intact building in Bonn large enough to house the assembly — and after being approved by the occupying powers on 12 May 1949, it was ratified by the parliaments of all the *Länder* with the exception of Bavaria (*Bayern*). The Landtag of Bavaria rejected the Basic Law mainly because it was seen as not granting sufficient powers to the individual Länder, but at the same time decided that it would still come into force in Bavaria if two-thirds of the other Länder ratified it. On 23 May 1949, the German Basic Law was promulgated and came into force a day later. The time of *legal nonentity* ended, as the new West German state, the Federal Republic of Germany, came into being.

Important differences from the Weimar Constitution

Basic rights are fundamental to the Basic Law, in contrast to the Weimar Constitution, which listed them merely as "state objectives." Pursuant to the mandate to respect human dignity, all state power is directly bound to guarantee these basic rights. Article 1 of the Basic Law (in German legal shorthand GG, for *Grundgesetz*), which establishes this principle that "human dignity is inviolable" and that human rights are directly applicable law, as well as the general principles of the state in Article 20 GG, which guarantees democracy, republicanism, social responsibility, federalism, and the right of resistance should anybody undertake to abolish this order, remain under the guarantee of perpetuity stated in Article 79 Paragraph 3, i.e., those two cannot be changed even if the normal amendment process is followed.

There are no emergency powers such as those used by the *Reichspräsident* in the Reichstag Fire Decree of 1933 to suspend basic rights and to remove communist members of the Reichstag from power, an important step for Hitler's *Machtergreifung*. The suspension of human rights would also be illegal under Articles 20 and 79 GG, as above.

The constitutional position of the federal government was strengthened, as the *Bundespräsident* has only a small fraction of the former power of the *Reichspräsident*. The government now depends only on the parliament.

To remove the chancellor, the parliament has to engage in a constructive vote of no confidence (*Konstruktives*

Misstrauensvotum), i.e. the election of a new chancellor. The new procedure was intended to provide more stability than under the Weimar Constitution, when extremists on the left and right would vote to remove a chancellor, without agreeing on a new one, creating a leadership vacuum. In addition it was possible for the parliament to remove individual ministers by a vote of distrust, while it now has to vote against the cabinet as a whole.

Article 32 of the Basic Law allows the states to conduct foreign affairs with states with regards to matters falling within their purview, under supervision of the Federal Government.

Article 24 states that the Federal Government may 'transfer sovereign powers to international institutions'.

Constitutional institutions

The Basic Law established Germany as a parliamentary democracy with separation of powers into executive, legislative, and judicial branches.

The executive branch consists of the largely ceremonial Federal President as head of state and the Federal Chancellor, the head of government, normally (but not necessarily) the leader of the largest grouping in the Bundestag.

The legislative branch is represented by the Bundestag, elected directly through a mixture of proportional representation and direct mandates, with the German *Länder* participating in legislation through the Bundesrat, reflecting Germany's federal structure.

The judicial branch is headed by the Federal Constitutional Court, which oversees the constitutionality of laws.

Presidency

The German *Bundespräsident* (federal president) is the head of state. It is a largely ceremonial position with only a minor role in day-to-day politics. Whereas the Weimar Constitution provided the president with far-reaching executive powers, the Federal President's main functions are representative and ceremonial, though as head of state he signs bills into laws and appoints federal officials. In contrast to the Weimar president, the new federal president can neither take the initiative to dissolve the Bundestag nor appoint a new chancellor without the consent of the Bundestag.

Executive branch

The Chancellor is the Head of government. They head the federal Cabinet, consisting of ministers appointed on the Chancellor's suggestion. While every minister governs his department autonomously, the Chancellor may issue overriding policy guidelines. The Chancellor is elected for a full term of the Bundestag and can only be dismissed by parliament electing a successor in a vote of no confidence.

Judicial branch

Federal Constitutional Court

The guardian of the Basic Law is the German Federal Constitutional Court (*Bundesverfassungsgericht*) which is both an independent constitutional organ and at the same time part of the judiciary in the sectors of constitutional law and public international law. Its judgements have the legal status of ordinary law. It can declare statutes as null and void if they are in violation of the Basic Law.

The court is famous for nullifying several high-profile laws, passed by large majorities in the parliament. An example is the Luftsicherheitsgesetz, which would have allowed the Bundeswehr to shoot down civilian aircraft in case of a terrorist attack. It was ruled to be in violation of the guarantee of life and human dignity in the Basic Law.

The Federal Constitutional Court decides on the constitutionality of laws and government actions under the following circumstances:

- individual complaint — a suit brought by a person alleging that a law or any action of government violated his or her constitutional rights. All possible solutions in the regular courts must have been exhausted beforehand.
- referral by regular court — a court can refer the question whether a statute applicable to the case before that court is constitutional.
- abstract regulation control — the federal government, a government of one of the federal states or a third of the Bundestag's members can bring suit against a law. In this case the suit need not refer to a specific case of the law's application.

The Weimar Constitution did not institute a court with similar powers. When the Basic Law is amended, this has to be done explicitly; the concerning article must be cited. Under Weimar the constitution could be amended without noticing; any law passed with a two-thirds majority vote was not bound by the constitution. Under the Basic Law, the fundamentals of the constitution in Art. 1 GG and Art. 20 GG, as well as elements of the federalist state, cannot be removed. Especially important is the protection of the division of state powers in the three branches, legislative, executive and judicial. This is provided by Art. 20 GG. A clear separation of powers was considered imperative to prevent measures like an over-reaching Enabling act, as happened in Germany in 1933. This act had then given the government legislative powers which effectively finished the Weimar Republic and led to the dictatorship of the Third Reich.

Other courts

Article 95 establishes the Federal Court of Justice, the Federal Administrative Court, the Federal Finance Court, the Federal Labour Court and the Federal Social Court as supreme courts in their respective areas of jurisdiction.

Article 96 authorises the establishment by federal law of the Federal Patent Court, of federal military criminal courts having jurisdiction only in a state of defence or on soldiers serving abroad, and of a federal disciplinary court. Article 92 establishes that all courts other than the federal courts established under the Basic Law are courts of the *Länder*.

Article 101 bans extraordinary courts, such as the *Volksgerichtshof*.

General provisions for the judiciary and rights of the accused

Article 97 provides for judicial independence. Article 102 abolishes capital punishment. Article 103 mandates a fair trial, forbids retroactive criminal legislation and multiple punishment for the same criminal act. Article 104 mandates that deprivation of personal liberty must be provided for by statute and authorised by a judge before the end of the day following the arrest (analogous to the common law concept of Habeas corpus), and that a relative or a person in the confidence of the prisoner must be notified of a judicial decision imposing detention.

Legislative branch

Bundestag

The main body of the legislative branch is Germany's parliament, the Bundestag, which enacts federal legislation, including the budget. Each member of the Bundestag has the right to initiate legislation, as do the cabinet and the Bundesrat. The Bundestag also elects the Chancellor, the head of government, usually (but not necessarily) the leader of the majority party or the party with a plurality of seats in the Bundestag, and takes part in the election of the Federal President.

Bundesrat

The Bundesrat represents the *Länder* (~States) and participates in federal legislation. The Bundesrat's power has grown over the years, as the fields of federal legislation were extended at the expense of state legislation. In return, the number of laws requiring the assent of the Bundesrat was also extended.

Role of political parties

In contrast to Weimar, political parties are explicitly mentioned in the constitution, i.e., officially recognized as important participants in politics. Parties are obliged to adhere to the democratic foundations of the German state. Parties found in violation of this requirement may be abolished by the constitutional court. In the Weimar Republic, the public image of political parties was clearly negative and they were often regarded as vile. At the same time there was no obligation to adhere to democratic standards (in contrast, the Basic Law stipulates that parties' "... internal organisation must conform to democratic principles", which precludes any party using the Führerprinzip, even internally.)

Other stipulations

Role of the military

The Weimar Constitution contributed to the Reichswehr becoming a state inside a state, outside of the control of the parliament or the public. The army directly reported to the president who himself was not dependent on the parliament. Under the Basic Law, during times of peace the Bundeswehr reports to the Minister of Defence, during time of war to the chancellor. The chancellor is directly responsible to the parliament, the Minister is indirectly responsible to the parliament because it can remove the entire Cabinet by electing a new chancellor. The Basic Law also institutes the parliamentary post of the *Wehrbeauftrager*, reporting to parliament not to the executive. The *Wehrbeauftrager* is a soldiers' ombudsman who can be petitioned directly by soldiers, bypassing the chain of command. Disciplinary measures against soldiers petitioning the *Wehrbeauftrager* are prohibited.

Although this is not explicitly spelled out in the Basic Law, a number of Constitutional Court cases in the 1990s established that the military may not be deployed by the government outside of NATO territory without a specific resolution of parliament, which describes the details of the mission and limits its term. There are also strict restrictions on the intervention of the military within Germany (i.e. a ban of the military being used for police-type duties), which generally only allow the military to act in unarmed roles within Germany (such as disaster relief).

Referendums and plebiscites

Unlike the Weimar Constitution, the Basic Law only allows referendums, concerning the federal level of legislation, on a single issue: a new delimitation of the federal territory. Baden-Württemberg was founded following a 1952 referendum that approved the fusion of three separate states. In a 1996 referendum the inhabitants of Berlin and Brandenburg rejected a proposed merger of the two states. After referendums on reestablishing to Länder borders as existed in the Weimar Republic all failed, this institution has not been used, as some little border changes can be done by state contract.

The denial of referendums in other cases was designed to avoid the kind of populism that allowed the rise of Hitler. Yet Article 20 states that "All state authority is derived from the people. It shall be exercised by the people through elections and other votes [*Abstimmungen*] and through specific legislative, executive and judicial bodies". These *other votes* – the words are to be understood meaning votes on legislative issues – are, by now, common practice on the level of the Länder. Claims of extending this practice also to the federal level have an undisputed constitutional basis in the Article 20, being *the* general and unchangeable article on state structure. However, this could only be conferred by a constitutional amendment nevertheless.

Development since 1949

Important changes to the Basic Law were the re-introduction of conscription and the establishment of the Bundeswehr in 1956. Therefore several articles were introduced into the constitution, e.g., Art. 12a, 17, 45a-c, 65a, 87a-c GG. Another important reform were the introduction in 1968 of emergency competences, for example Art. 115 Paragraph 1 GG. This was done by a grand coalition of the two main political parties CDU/CSU and SPD and was accompanied by heated debate. In the following year there were changes to the articles regarding the distribution of taxes between federal government and the states of Germany.

During reunification, the two states

discussed the possibility of drafting a new common constitution followed by a plebiscite, as envisioned in Art. 146 (1990), but this path was ultimately not taken. Instead the Federal Republic of Germany and the German Democratic Republic decided to keep the Basic Law with only minor changes, because it had proved to be effective in West Germany. To facilitate reunification and to reassure other states, the FRG made some changes to the Basic Law. Article 23 was fulfilled by reunification itself, and then withdrawn to indicate that there were no other parts of Germany that existed outside of the unified territory. The question of "using" Article 146 to draw a new constitution, and hold a referendum, was left to the twelfth (and first all-German) Bundestag, who after considering the question decided against a new draft. However, the Bundestag passed the constitutional reform of 1994, a minor change, but still fulfilling the constitutional question together with some other amendments between 1990 and 1994. For example, affirmative action was allowed in women's rights, and environmental protection was made a policy objective of the state in the new Article 20a. In 1992, membership in the European Union was institutionalised (Art. 23 GG). For the privatisation of the railways and the postal service, amendments were necessary as well. Since then, there have only been minor amendments. In 2002, protection of animals was explicitly mentioned in Art. 20a GG.

The most controversial debate arose concerning the limitation of the right to asylum in 1993 as in the current version of Art. 16 a GG. This change was later challenged and confirmed in a judgment by the constitutional court. Another controversy was spawned by the limitation of the right to the invulnerability of the private domain (*Unverletzlichkeit der Wohnung*) by means of acoustic observation (*Großer Lauschangriff*). This was done by changes to Art. 13 Paragraph 3 and Art. 6 GG. The changes were challenged in the constitutional court, but the judges confirmed the changes. Other changes took place regarding a redistribution of competencies between federal government and the *Länder*.

Early elections

The Basic Law contains no clear provision to call early elections. Neither the chancellor nor the Bundestag has the power to call elections, and the president can do so only if the government loses a confidence vote if the chancellor so requests. This was designed to avoid the chronic instability of Weimar Republic governments. However, early elections have been called three times (1972, 1982, and 2005). On the last two occasions this was a controversial move and was referred to the constitutional court for review.

In 1972, Chancellor Willy Brandt's coalition had lost its majority in the Bundestag, so that the opposition CDU/CSU tried to do a constructive vote of no confidence, thus electing Rainer Barzel as new chancellor. Surprisingly, two representative of CDU/CSU voted for SPD's Willy Brandt, so that the vote failed. Nevertheless, the coalition had no majority in the Bundestag, so that a new election was necessary. (Later it turned out that the GDR secret service had bribed the two dissenting representatives.)

In 1982, Chancellor Helmut Kohl intentionally lost a confidence vote in order to call an early election to strengthen his position in the Bundestag. The constitutional court examined the case, and decided that the vote was valid, but with reservations. It was decided that a vote of no confidence could be engineered only if it were based on an actual legislative impasse.

In 2005, Chancellor Gerhard Schröder engineered a defeat in a motion of no confidence after a power shift in the *Bundesrat*. President Horst Köhler then called elections for 18 September 2005. The constitutional court agreed to the validity of this procedure on August 25, 2005, and the elections duly took place.

Source (edited): "http://en.wikipedia.org/wiki/Basic_Law_for_the_Federal_Republic_of_Germany"

Federal Constitutional Court of Germany

The Bundesverfassungsgericht

The **Federal Constitutional Court** (in German: *Bundesverfassungsgericht*, or *BVerfG*) is a special court established by the *Grundgesetz*, the German basic law. Since its inception, the constitutional court has been located in the city of Karlsruhe, intentionally dislocated from the other federal institutions like the seat of the government in Berlin (earlier in Bonn), the head office of the BND (the German foreign intelligence agency) near Munich, or the seat of the Bundesbank (central bank) in Frankfurt.

The sole task of the court is judicial review. It may therefore declare public acts unconstitutional and thus render them ineffective. As such, it is similar to the Supreme Court of the United States. Yet the Court possesses a number of powers that the U.S. Supreme Court does not have (see below). It also differs from the U.S. and other supreme courts in that it is not an integral part of the regular judicial system (save for the areas of constitutional law and public international law) but installed as a separate judicial institution. Many other countries around the world possess separate constitutional courts similar to the Federal Constitutional Court.

Most importantly, the Court does not

serve as a regular appellate court from lower courts or the Federal Supreme Courts as a sort of "superappellate court" on any violation of federal laws. Its jurisdiction is focused on constitutional issues, the integrity of the *Grundgesetz* and the immediate compliance of any governmental institution in any detail (article 1 subsection 3 of the *Grundgesetz*). Even constitutional amendments or changes passed by the Parliament are subject to its judicial review, since they have to be compatible with the most basic principles of the *Grundgesetz* (due to its Article 79 (III), the so called 'eternity clause').

The court's practice of enormous constitutional control frequency on the one hand, and the continuity in judicial restraint and political revision on the other hand, have created a unique defender of the *Grundgesetz* since World War II and given it a valuable role in Germany's modern democracy.

Procedures

Article 20 subsection 3 of the *Grundgesetz* stipulates that all the three branches of the state—legislative, executive and judicial—are bound directly by the constitution. As a result, the court can rule acts of any branches unconstitutional, whether for formal violations (exceeding powers or violating procedures) or for material conflicts (when the civil rights prescribed in the *Grundgesetz* are not respected).

The powers of the Federal Constitutional Court are defined in article 93 of the *Grundgesetz*. This constitutional norm is concertized by a federal law, the Federal Constitutional Court Act (BVerfGG). This federal law also defines how decisions of the court on material conflicts are put into force.

The Constitutional Court has therefore several strictly defined procedures in which cases may be brought before it:

- With a **Constitutional Complaint** (*Verfassungsbeschwerde*), any person may allege that his or her constitutional rights were violated. Although only a small fraction of these are actually successful (ranging around 2.5 % since 1951), several of these resulted in major legislation being thrown out, especially in the field of taxation. The large majority of the court's procedures fall in this category, with 135,968 such Complaints filed from 1957 to 2002.
- Several political institutions, including the governments of the *Bundesländer*, may bring a federal law before the court if they consider it unconstitutional (procedure of **Abstract Regulation Control**). The most well-known examples of these procedures included legislation legalizing abortion, which—in highly debated rulings—were declared unconstitutional twice by the Constitutional Court.
- Any regular court which is convinced, that a law in question for a certain case is not in conformance with the constitution must suspend that case and bring this law before the Federal Constitutional Court (procedure of **Specific Regulation Control**).
- Federal institutions, including members of the Bundestag, may bring internal disputes over competences and procedures before the court (**Federal Dispute**).
- The *Länder* may bring disputes over competences and procedures between them and federal institutions before the court (**State-Federal Dispute**).
- Committee on parliament investigation, including single members of the *Bundestag*, or the federal government may bring internal disputes over competences and procedures in case of committee's investigation before the court (**Investigation Committee Control**).
- Violations of election laws may be brought before the court by political institution or any involved voter (**Federal Election Scrutiny**).
- Impeachment cases against the President or a judge, member of one of the Federal Supreme Courts, brought by the Bundestag, the Bundesrat or the federal government, based on violation of constitutional or federal law (**Impeachment Procedure**).
- Finally, only the Constitutional Court has the power to **prohibit a political party** in Germany. This has happened just twice, both times in the 1950s: the Socialist Reich Party (*Sozialistische Reichspartei*, SRP), an outright neo-Nazi party, was banned in 1952, and the Communist Party of Germany (*Kommunistische Partei Deutschlands*, KPD) was banned in 1956. A third such procedure to prohibit the far-right National Democratic Party of Germany (NPD) failed in 2003 after the court discovered that many of the party officials were in fact controlled by the German secret services that had injected its agents for the sake of surveillance. This was a 4-4 decision, which according to the court's rules is considered a dismissal. The court did not decide on the ban itself.

Organization

First Senate 1989

Second Senate 1989

The Court consists of two Senates, each of which has eight members, headed by a senate's chairman. The members of each Senate are allocated to three Chambers for hearings in Constitutional Complaint and Single Regulation Control cases. Each Chamber consists of three judges, so each Senate chairman is at the same time a member of two Chambers.

Decisions by a Senate require an absolute majority. In some cases a two thirds majority is required (§ 15 IV 1 BVerfGG). Decisions by a Chamber need to be unanimous. A Chamber is not authorized to overrule a standing precedent of the Senate to which it belongs; such issues need to be submitted to the Senate as a whole. Similarly, a Senate may not overrule a standing precedent of the other Senate; such issues will be submitted to a plenary meeting of all 16 judges (the "Plenum").

Unlike all other German courts, the court often publishes the vote count on its decisions (though only the final tally, not every judge's personal vote) and even allows its members to issue a dissenting opinion. This possibility, introduced only in 1971, is a remarkable deviation from German judicial tradition.

One of the two Senate Chairmen is also the President of the Court, the other one being the Vice-President. The presidency alternates between the two Senates, i.e. the successor of a President is always chosen from the other Senate. The current president of the Court is Andreas Voßkuhle.

Election of judges

The Court's judges are elected by the Bundestag and the Bundesrat. According to the Basic Law, each of these bodies selects four members of each Senate, while the authority to select the Court's President alternates between them. The selection of a judge requires a two-thirds majority.

The Bundestag has delegated this task to a special body ("Richterwahlausschuss", *judges election board*), consisting of a small number of Bundestag members. This procedure has caused some constitutional concern and is considered to be unconstitutional by many scholars. However, it has never been challenged in a court.

The judges are elected for a 12-year term, but they must retire when reaching the age of 68. A judge must be at least 40 years old and must be a well-trained jurist. Three out of eight members of each Senate must have served as a judge of a Federal Supreme Court. Of the other five members of each Senate, most judges previously served as a professor of law at a University, a public servant or an attorney. After ending their term, most judges withdraw themselves from public life. However, there are some prominent exceptions, most notably Roman Herzog, who was elected Federal President in 1994, shortly before the end of his term as President of the Court.

Presidents of the Court
- Hermann Höpker-Aschoff

Source (edited): "http://en.wikipedia.org/wiki/Federal_Constitutional_Court_of_Germany"

German Federal Constitutional Court abortion decision

The Federal Constitutional Court of Germany addressed the issue of abortion in 1975, two years after *Roe v. Wade*, in a decision reported at BVerfGE 39,1, holding that respect for human dignity requires the criminalization of abortion.

Notably, it said that the state has a duty to use "social, political, and welfare means" to foster developing human life, and that these are preferable to penal measures (though the latter are not ruled out). The decision came several years after decisions in the U.S. and Britain legalized abortion. It struck down a law that legalized some abortions in the first three months.

The decision considered the full range of arguments for abortion, both early (legalization had been a topic of debate in Germany since the turn of the century) and recent (used in other countries such as the United States and Britain that legalized abortion several years before). In particular, it specifically rejected the main points of reasoning in *Roe v. Wade* as well as its "term solution" as inconsistent with the constitutional guarantee of the right to life.

The Court held that Article 2, Paragraph 2 of the Basic Law for the Federal Republic of Germany's guarantee that "Everyone has the right to life", read in light of Article 1's guarantee of human dignity, must extend to the life of the unborn.

The reunification of Germany resulted in a significant revision of abortion laws, which liberalized them in many respects, although leaving them more restrictive than the East German laws which permitted abortion upon demand during the first twelve weeks of pregnancy. In a separate decision in 1992, the Federal Constitutional Court upheld the relaxed restrictions on abortion.

The decision does not make all abortions punishable, however. In the early 1990s, the German legislature (Bundestag) implemented a system where a woman having an abortion during the first three months of her pregnancy does not face legal sanctions if she undergoes mandatory counseling which has as one of its goals to present the case that the developing fetus is an independent human life, and obeys a 72 hour waiting period between counseling and the abortion. Later abortions are not punishable if medical reasons, such as possible harm to the woman from continued pregnancy, or a severely deformed fetus, indicate so. Despite some of the reasoning contained in the original German supreme court decision, the court has not found this system to conflict with the constitution. Some abortions are therefore illegal, but not punishable – de facto legal.

A significant number of abortions in fact occur in Germany, but the incidence per capita is about one-fifth that of the United States.

Source (edited): "http://en.wikipedia.org/wiki/German_Federal_Constitutional_Court_abortion_decision"

Herrenchiemsee convention

The **constitutional convention at Herrenchiemsee** (*Verfassungskonvent auf Herrenchiemsee*) was a meeting held in 1948 in the Herrenchiemsee complex in Bavaria, West Germany, as part of the process of adopting the current German constitution, the Basic Law (*Grundgesetz*).

Source (edited): "http://en.wikipedia.org/wiki/Herrenchiemsee_convention"

Streitbare Demokratie

The political system of the Federal Republic of Germany is also called **wehrhafte** or **streitbare Demokratie (fortified democracy)**. This implies that the government (Bundesregierung), the parliament (Bundestag) and the judiciary are given extensive powers to defend the **freiheitlich-demokratische Grundordnung (liberal democratic order)** against those who want to abolish it. The idea behind the concept is the notion that even a majority of the people cannot be allowed to install a totalitarian or autocratic regime, thereby violating the principles of the German constitution, the Basic Law.

Tools of the 'Streitbare Demokratie'

Several articles of the German constitution allow a range of different measures to "defend the liberal democratic order".

- Art. 9 allows for social groups to be labelled "verfassungsfeindlich" ("hostile to the constitution") and to be prohibited by the federal government. Political parties can only be labelled enemies to the constitution by Germany's highest court, the Bundesverfassungsgericht (federal constitutional court), according to Art. 21 II.
- According to Art. 18, the Bundesverfassungsgericht can restrict the basic rights of people who fight against the "verfassungsgemäße Ordnung" (constitutional order). As of 2008, this has never happened in the history of the Federal Republic.
- The federal and state bureaucracies can exclude people deemed "hostile to the constitution" from the civil service according to Art. 33. Every civil servant is sworn to defend the constitution and the constitutional order (Berufsverbot).
- According to Art. 20, every German citizen has the right to resistance against anyone who wants to abolish the constitutional order, though only as a last resort.

Source (edited): "http://en.wikipedia.org/wiki/Streitbare_Demokratie"

Andreas Voßkuhle

Andreas Voßkuhle (born 21 December 1963) is a German legal scholar and the president of the Federal Constitutional Court of Germany.

Life

Voßkuhle started studying law at the Ludwig Maximilian University of Munich between 1983 and 1989. In 1989 he passed the first Staatsexamen. Before he completed the second Staatsexamen in 1993 he wrote his doctoral thesis (German title *Rechtsschutz gegen den Richter*) under supervision of Peter Lerche.

Between 1992 and 1994 he was a research fellow at the chair for public law in Augsburg. Later, in 1995, he worked as a referent in the Ministry of the Interior of the Free State of Bavaria. Following his habilitation at the University of Augsburg in 1998, he became a full professor at the University of Freiburg in 1999 as well as the head of their institute for political science and the philosophy of law. At this university he held various positions, e. g. the one of the faculty director of the law faculty in the following years.

Since 2007 he is also an ordinary member of the Berlin-Brandenburg Academy of Sciences and Humanities. Later, in July 2007, he became the head of the University of Freiburg as well. He started to work in this position in April 2008.

In May 2008, Voßkuhle became the vice-president of the Federal Constitutional Court of Germany and the chairman of its second senate. He was the second choice of the SPD, after their initial candidate, Horst Dreier, was rejected by the CDU because of his position regarding stem cell research and torture. When the mandate of the former President of the Court, Hans-Jürgen Papier ended in 2010, Voßkuhle became the youngest President in the history of the Federal Constitutional Court of Germany.
Source (edited): "http://en.wikipedia.org/wiki/Andreas_Vo%C3%9Fkuhle"

Brun-Otto Bryde

Brun-Otto Bryde (* 1943) is a German legal scholar and a former judge of the Federal Constitutional Court of Germany.

Life

Bryde was born in Hamburg on January 12, 1943. Following his first state exam in law 1966 and his second one in 1969 he did his doctoral degree in Hamburg in 1971. After that he became an instructor at a university in Ethiopia. Between 1973 and 1974 he was a Law and Modernization Fellow at the Yale Law School. Later, from 1974 until 1982, he was a teacher at the university of Hamburg. 1980 he did his habilitation and afterwards he became a professor at Bundeswehr University of Munich. Since 1987 he is a professor at the University of Giessen. He was a visiting professor two times at the university of Wisconsin law school in 1989 and 1994 as well. Bryde was also a member of the Committee on the Elimination of All Forms of Racial Discrimination. From 2001 to 2011 he was a judge at the Federal Constitutional Court of Germany (1st. Senate). He was the first judge of the Federal Constitutional Court to be elected on the proposal of the Green party. He was followed by judge Susanne Baer.
Source (edited): "http://en.wikipedia.org/wiki/Brun-Otto_Bryde"

Christine Hohmann-Dennhardt

Christine Hohmann-Dennhardt (born 30 April 1950) is a German politician and senior judge.

Biography

After being a lecturer for Labour at the University of Hamburg from 1975 to 1977, she became a researcher at the Johann Wolfgang Goethe University in Frankfurt am Main. She earned her doctorate there in 1979.

From 1981 to 1984 she was a judge at the *Sozialgerichten* ("Social Courts") in Frankfurt am Main and Wiesbaden and the *Landessozialgericht* ("Country Social Courts") of Hessen. In 1984 she was appointed Director of the Wiesbaden *Sozialgerichten* and remained in that position until 1989. From 1988 to 1989 she was also a substitute member of the Hessen State Constitutional Court, *Staatsgerichtshof des Landes Hessen*.

From 1989 to 1991 she was a *Dezernentin der Stadt* (roughly, "City Councillor") of Frankfurt am Main. In 1991 she was appointed Minister of Justice in the Hessen state government. From 1995 to 1999 she served as Minister of Science and Arts.

From January 1999 to January 2011 she sat on the First Senate of the *Bundesverfassungsgericht* (Federal Constitutional Court of Germany). When Evelyn Haas left the *Bundesverfassungsgericht* in 2006, Hohmann-Dennhardt was the only woman on the First Senate. In January 2011, Hohmann-Dennhardt was followed by judge Gabriele Britz.

In May 2001 she became a member of the *Hochschulrates* (roughly, "Board of Trustees") of the University of Karlsruhe.
Source (edited): "http://en.wikipedia.org/wiki/Christine_Hohmann-Dennhardt"

Erna Scheffler

Erna Scheffler, born **Friedental** and later **Haßlacher** (born 21 September 1893 in Wroclaw, died 22 May 1983 in London) was a German senior judge.

Education and early career

She attended the girls' schools in Legnica and Wroclaw and gained her baccalaureate in 1911 in Racibórz. She studied for a semester at Heidelberg University and then switched from medicine to law in Wroclaw, Munich and Berlin. In December 1914 she finished her studies with a doctorate from Wroclaw. Women were not yet permitted to take the state legal exams, so she initially worked in social welfare and then as an assistant at a law practice. She married for the first time in 1916, and lived in Belgium until 1918, where her husband worked as a lawyer in the German civil administration. After the First World War, she found employment with the *Bund Deutscher Architekten* ((German) "Association of German Architects") and various law firms.

Women were allowed to take the law exams in 1921, and Scheffler became a clerk in 1922. Between then and 1925, when she graduated as a full lawyer, she divorced her first husband. From late 1925 to 1928 she was a lawyer in certain Berlin districts before moving to the Assenburg Sorin Court in 1930. From 1932 she was a permanent relief worker at the District Court.

Nazi Germany

In November 1933, she was found to be "non-Aryan" and received an employment ban that was backdated to 1 March 1933. She received only a small pension. Her second marriage, to George Scheffler, was denied in 1934 because she was *Halbjüdin* ((German) "half-Jewish"). She worked as an accountant in a friend's business and distributed food during the war. From January 1945 until the end of the war, she hid in a *Gartenhäuschen* ((German) "little garden house") outside Berlin.

After the war

Immediately after the war she married George Scheffler and returned in May 1945, first as Regional Councillor and later as Regional Director of the *Landgericht Berlin* ((German) "Regional Court of Berlin") in the Justice Service. After the 1948 currency reform, she became a Councillor in the Düsseldorf *Verwaltungsgericht* ((German) "Administrative Court"). On the German "Judges' Day" in 1950, she gave an address about equality between men and women, and was thus recommended as a Federal Judge. In September 1951 she was the only woman in the German Federal Constitutional Court in Karlsruhe, serving as a judge there until 1963. Thereafter, she was an expert for the Interior Committee of the German Bundestag. She died in 1983 at her daughter's house in London.
Source (edited): "http://en.wikipedia.org/wiki/Erna_Scheffler"

Ernst-Wolfgang Böckenförde

Ernst-Wolfgang Böckenförde

Ernst-Wolfgang Böckenförde (born September 19, 1930 in Kassel) is a German judge and legal philosopher.

Life

In 1953 he received a PhD in law as well as in philosophy. In 1964 he made his postdoctoral habilitation with his thesis *The power of organisation in the purview of the government. A survey on constitutional law in the Federal Republic of Germany*. Ernst-Wolfgang Böckenförde was a judge in the Federal Constitutional Court of Germany from 1983 to 1996.

Ernst-Wolfgang Böckenförde served as a member of the second Senate of the Federal Constitutional Court from 1982 until 1996. Into his tenure fall several path-breaking decisions for the Federal Republic of Germany, including decisions pertaining to the deployment of missiles, to the law of political parties, and to the legal regulation of abortion.

After receiving a Dr. iur. and a Dr. phil., he completed his habilitation in Münster in 1964. Ernst-Wolfgang Böckenförde has taught as a professor of Public Law, Constitutional History, Legal History, Philosophy of Law at the University of Heidelberg, the University of Bielefeld and the University of Freiburg.

Böckenförde was a member of the Special Parliamentary Commission of Inquiry on Constitutional Reform. He has received various awards for his academic and public service commitments: Honorary Doctorates from the Faculties of Catholic Theology of Bochum University (1999) and of Tübingen University (2005), from the Law Schools of Bielefeld University (1999), of the University of Münster (2001) and of the University of Basel (1987).

He is most famous for his quote: "The liberal secular state lives on premises that it cannot itself guarantee. On the one hand, it can subsist only if the freedom it consents to its citizens is regulated from within, inside the moral substance of individuals and of a homogeneous society. On the other hand, it is not able to guarantee these forces of inner regulation by itself without renouncing its liberalism."

He has also received the Reuchlin Award of the City of Pforzheim (1978), the Guardini Award of the Catholic Academy in Bavaria (2004) and the Hannah-Arendt Award for Political Thought (2004).
Source (edited): "http://en.wikipedia.org/wiki/Ernst-Wolfgang_B%C3%B6ckenf%C3%B6rde"

Ernst Benda

Ernst Benda (15 January 1925 – 2 March 2009) was a German legal scholar, politician and judge. He served as the 4th president of the Federal Constitutional Court of Germany from 1971 to 1983. Benda briefly served as Minister of the Interior of Germany (1968 to 1969).

Ernst Benda was born in Berlin, the son of an Engineer. After school he served in the Kriegsmarine from 1943 to 1945. After the war he studied law at the Humboldt University of Berlin in East Berlin, but in 1948 moved to the University of Wisconsin–Madison and then to the Free University of Berlin in West Berlin. 1956 he started to work as a lawyer in Berlin.

From 1946 Benda was member of the Christian Democratic Union (CDU). From 1954 to 1957 he was member of the Abgeordnetenhaus von Berlin, the parliament of Berlin. 1957 he was elected to the Bundestag, the West German parliament. In 1965 he was involved in bringing significant changes to West Germany's statutes of limitations for murder. Without these changes it would not have been possible to bring charges of murder against erstwhile National Socialists. Since 1967 he was Secretary of State in the German interior ministry and since 1968 Minister of the Interior. 1969 he was appointed as a judge to the Federal Constitutional Court of Germany. From 1971 to 1983 he was president of the court. From 1984 Benda was professor of law at the University of Freiburg.

Awards and honours

1974 Grand Cross of Merit of the Italian Republic
1975 Grand Gold Medal with Ribbon for Services to the Republic of Austria
1983 Grand Cross of the Order of Merit of the Federal Republic of Germany
1974 Honorary Doctorate from the Faculty of Law, Julius-Maximilians-Universität Würzburg
1978 Honorary Professor at the University of Trier
1978 Pipe smoker of the year
1987 Heinz-Herbert Karry Prize
Source (edited): "http://en.wikipedia.org/wiki/Ernst_Benda"

Ernst Träger

Ernst Träger (born January 29, 1926) is a German judge. He was a judge in the Federal Constitutional Court of Germany between 1977 and 1989.
Source (edited): "http://en.wikipedia.org/wiki/Ernst_Tr%C3%A4ger"

Evelyn Haas

Evelyn Haas, born **Evelyn Traeger** (born 7 April 1949) is a German former First Senate Constitutional Court judge and current Honorary Professor of Law. She was the first woman to be elected to the Constitutional Court in Germany.

Biography

After receiving her doctorate in 1974, Haas became a judge in Lower Saxony. She was at the Administrative Court for ten months, then seconded to the local government in Wolfsburg. From 1982 to 1986 she was seconded as a research assistant at the Federal Government of Germany and from 1986 to 1990, a judge at the Higher Administrative Court of Lüneburg. From 1987 to 1990 she was also Head of Unit in the Lower Saxony State Chancellery.

From September 1994 she was in the First Senate of the *Bundesverfassungsgericht* (Federal Constitutional Court of Germany). Her twelve-year term ended in 2006 and Wilhelm Schluckebier succeeded her.

She was responsible for certain areas of German tax law, development law, construction law, land law, the German expropriation law, land transport and urban development. She was a planning law specialist, except for environment law. She had input on several landmark case law decisions, sometimes dissenting from her colleagues.

With her departure, only one woman (Christine Hohmann-Dennhardt) sat on the German First Senate. This led to a debate about whether women are still at a disadvantage in the German legal system.

Since 2002 she has taught as an Honorary Professor at Eberhard-Karls-Universität, Tübingen.
Source (edited): "http://en.wikipedia.org/wiki/Evelyn_Haas"

Everhardt Franßen

Everhardt Franßen

Everhardt Franßen (born October 1, 1937 in Essen) is a retired German judge. He was a judge in the Federal Constitutional Court of Germany and the Federal Administrative Court of Germany, presiding the latter one between 1991 and 2002.
Source (edited): "http://en.wikipedia.org/wiki/Everhardt_Fran%C3%9Fen"

Ferdinand Kirchhof

Ferdinand Kirchhof (born June 21, 1950 in Osnabrück) is a German judge, jurisprudent and tax law expert. Since October 1st, 2007, he is sitting Justice of the Federal Constitutional Court of Germany in the court's first senate. In March 2009, he has been elected vice president of the court. Kirchhof is the younger brother of former Justice of the Federal Constitutional Court of Germany Paul Kirchhof.
Source (edited): "http://en.wikipedia.org/wiki/Ferdinand_Kirchhof"

Franz Wessel

Wessel in 1951

Franz Wessel (March 6, 1903 - September 10, 1958) was a German judge. He was a judge in the Federal Constitutional Court of Germany in the 1950s.

Source (edited): "http://en.wikipedia.org/wiki/Franz_Wessel"

Gebhard Müller

Gebhard Müller (April 17, 1900 – August 7, 1990) was a German lawyer and politician (CDU). He was Minister-President of Württemberg-Hohenzollern (1948-1952) and Baden-Württemberg (1953-1958). He was born in Füramoos and died in Stuttgart.
Source (edited): "http://en.wikipedia.org/wiki/Gebhard_M%C3%BCller"

Gertrude Lübbe-Wolff

Gertrude Lübbe-Wolff (born 31 January 1953) is a German academic and senior judge. She sits on the second senate of the *Bundesverfassungsgericht* (Federal Constitutional Court of Germany), having succeeded Jutta Limbach in this position in April 2002.

Biography

After studying law at the University of Bielefeld, the Albert-Ludwigs-Universität in Freiburg and Harvard Law School, Lübbe-Wolff received her doctorate in law at Freiburg im Breisgau. From 1979 to 1987 she was a research assistant at Bielefeld, focusing on public law, the constitutional history of the modern age, and philosophy of law. From 1988 to 1992 she was director of the *Wasserschutzamt* ("Water Office") in Bielefeld, before being called to a professorship in Public Law, again at the University of Bielefeld.

In 2000 Lübbe-Wolff received the Gottfried Wilhelm Leibniz Prize of the *Deutsche Forschungsgemeinschaft* (the highest German prize for research).

She is married to the philosopher Michael Wolff and has four children. Her father and both of her sisters are all university professors.

Selected publications

Translator's note: These are all in German, except the last.

Monographs

- *Die Grundrechte als Eingriffsabwehrrechte. Baden-Baden (Nomos) 1988.* ("Fundamental Rights as a Defensive Action")
- *Recht und Moral im Umweltschutz. Baden-Baden (Nomos) 1999.* ("Law and Morality in the Environment")

Editorships

- *Umweltschutz durch Kommunales Satzungsrecht. Berlin (Erich Schmidt) 1993 - 2. Auflage 1997.* ("Municipal Environmental Protection by Statute Law")
- *Symbolische Umweltpolitik (zusammen mit Bernd Hansjürgens). Frankfurt a.M. (Suhrkamp) 2000.* ("Symbolic Political Environment")
- *Effizientes Umweltordnungsrecht – Kriterien und Grenzen (with Erik Gawel). Baden-Baden (Nomos) 2000.* ("Efficient Environmental Regulatory Law – Criteria and Limits")

Essays

- *Globalisierung und Demokratie. Überlegungen am Beispiel der Wasserwirtschaft, in: Recht und Politik 3/2004, S. 130 - 143.* ("Globalisation and Democracy. Reflections on the Example of Water Management.")
- *Substantiierung und Subsidiarität der Verfassungsbeschwerde, in: EuGRZ 2004, S. 669 - 682.* ("Substantiation and Subsidiarity in the Constitution")
- *Die erfolgreiche Verfassungsbeschwerde, Anwaltsblatt 2005, S. 509 ff.* ("The Successful Verfassungsbeschwerde")
- *Homogenes Volk – über Homogenitätspostulate und Integration, in: ZAR 2007, S. 121-127.* ("Homogenous People – on the Postulates of Homogenity and Integration")

Papers

- Humboldt Forum Recht, "ECtHR and national jurisdiction - The Görgülü Case", together with the European Convention on Human Rights.

Source (edited): "http://en.wikipedia.org/wiki/Gertrude_L%C3%BCbbe-Wolff"

Hans-Jürgen Papier

Hans-Jürgen Papier (German pronunciation: [ˈpaːpiɐ]; born 6 July 1943 in Berlin) is a German scholar of constitutional law and was President of the Federal Constitutional Court of Germany from 2002 to 2010.

Three years after graduating from law school in 1967 with the first law state examination, Papier completed his Ph.D. studies at the Freie Universität Berlin. In 1971 he received the second law state examination. In 1973 he received his *Habilitation* on the basis of a second dissertation on questions concerning German constitutional law.

From 1974 onward Papier received tenure at the Universität Bielefeld and taught constitutional law. In 1992 he moved to Munich to teach German and Bavarian constitutional and administrative law as well as Public Social law at the Ludwig-Maximilians-Universität.

In 1998 Papier, a member of the conservative CSU party, became Vice-President and Chair of the First Senate of the Federal Constitutional Court of Germany. When Chief Justice Jutta Limbach retired from her position in 2002, Papier succeeded her.

Papier has often made public comments on questions of constitutional law, but has generally avoided commenting on other political questions. He made an exception to this rule after the elections of 2005 when he implored the parties to work hard not to lose the trust of the German electorate.

Source (edited): "http://en.wikipedia.org/wiki/Hans-J%C3%BCrgen_Papier"

Hans Georg Rupp

Rupp in 1951

Hans Georg Rupp (August 30, 1907 - September 14, 1989) was a German judge. He was a judge in the Federal Constitutional Court of Germany from 1951 to 1975.
Source (edited): "http://en.wikipedia.org/wiki/Hans_Georg_Rupp"

Hans Hugo Klein

Hans Hugo Klein (born August 5, 1936 in Karlsruhe) is a German politician, representative of the German Christian Democratic Union from 1983 to 1996 and was judge at the Constitutional Court.

Life

Klein studied law in Heidelberg and Munich, where in 1961 his Ph.D. graduated. Then he moved to the Management Service of Baden-Wuerttemberg, lost but not the scientific career from his eyes, which led 1967 Habilitation on the topic "Participation of the state in economic competition with Ernst Forsthoff at the University of Heidelberg. 1969 Hans Hugo Klein took a call to a professorship for Public Law at the University of Göttingen. In 1970 he joined the CDU, for which he belonged from 1972 to 1983 the German Bundestag. He moved in 1972, 1976 and 1980, one of the Land of Lower Saxony CDU in parliament, winning 1983, the direct mandate in the constituency of Göttingen.

From 1982 to 1983 he was among Hans A. Engelhard also Parliamentary Secretary in the Ministry of Justice.

In 1983 he was appointed as a judge of the Constitutional Court. During his tenure at the Federal Small belonged to the Second Senate of the court. His responsibilities with the Federal Party were right, the right of the public service and staff representation rights. He was succeeded by Hans-Joachim Jentsch.

For constitutional matters Hans Hugo Klein believes that it is acting in the Basic Law for a mixed constitution. Mixed is the democratic constitutional state in the Federal Republic of Germany, since democracy is not absolutely true. Particular importance come to the concept of representative democracy. The political parties were in the process, despite the criticism is often practiced in them, constitutionally necessary component of liberal democracy.
Source (edited): "http://en.wikipedia.org/wiki/Hans_Hugo_Klein"

Helga Seibert

Helga Seibert (January 7, 1939 in Witzenhausen - April 12, 1999) was a German judge. She was a judge in the Federal Constitutional Court of Germany.

Shortly before her death she won the Fritz Bauer Prize from the Humanist Union. The explanatory memorandum stated; "The fact that a civil rights organization honors a supreme judge, may seem unusual, but it is for your work towards the specific benefits of dealing with fundamental rights."

Source (edited): "http://en.wikipedia.org/wiki/Helga_Seibert"

Hermann Höpker-Aschoff

Hermann Höpker-Aschoff (31 January 1883 - 15 January 1954) was a German politician and jurist. He was the first President of the Federal Constitutional Court of Germany.

Höpker-Aschoff studied law and economics at the University of Jena, and taught monetary theory and finance as professor at the University of Bonn.

Source (edited): "http://en.wikipedia.org/wiki/Hermann_H%C3%B6pker-Aschoff"

Johannes Masing

Johannes Masing (born January 9, 1959 in Wiesbaden) is a German judge, jurisprudent and public law scholar. On February 15th, 2008, he succeeded Wolfgang Hoffmann-Riem as sitting Justice of the Federal Constitutional Court of Germany in the court's first senate.

Source (edited): "http://en.wikipedia.org/wiki/Johannes_Masing"

Josef Wintrich

Josef Marquard Wintrich (February 15, 1891 – October 19, 1958) was a German legal scholar and judge. He served as the 2nd president of the Federal Constitutional Court of Germany from 1954 to 1956. The most significant decision during his tenure was the banning of the Communist Party of Germany in 1956.

Source (edited): "http://en.wikipedia.org/wiki/Josef_Wintrich"

Jutta Limbach

Jutta Limbach (born March 27, 1934 in Berlin) is a German jurist and politician. She is a member of the Social Democratic Party of Germany (SPD). She received her doctorate in law in 1966 by the Free University of Berlin and fulfilled the requirements to be appointed professor by the German educational system in 1971. In 1972, she was appointed professor of private law at the Free University. From 1987 to 1989, she was member of an academic advisory council at the Federal Ministry for Family Affairs, Senior Citizens, Women and Youth. Under Walter Momper as mayor, Limbach was the senator for Justice in Berlin from 1989 to 1994. In 1994, she was then appointed to the position of vice-president of the Federal Constitutional Court of Germany, the same year she became president, succeeding Roman Herzog. She was the first female president of the court and served in this role until she reached the age limit of 68 in 2002. She then became president of the German non-profit organization Goethe-Institut. In 2004, she was repeatedly named as a possible candidate to succeed Johannes Rau as President of Germany in that year's election. Limbach is a member of the committee of the Peace Prize of the German Book Trade. In 2005, she was awarded the Louise-Schroeder-Medal.

Source (edited): "http://en.wikipedia.org/wiki/Jutta_Limbach"

Jürgen Kühling

Jürgen Kühling (born April 27, 1934 in Osnabrück) is a German judge. He was a judge in the Federal Constitutional Court of Germany between 1989 and 2001.
Source (edited): "http://en.wikipedia.org/wiki/J%C3%BCrgen_K%C3%BChling"

Karin Graßhof

Karin Graßhof (born June 25, 1937 in Kiel) is a German jurist. She served as a judge at the Federal Constitutional Court of Germany from 1986 to 1998. She is currently an honourary professor at the University of Bonn
Source (edited): "http://en.wikipedia.org/wiki/Karin_Gra%C3%9Fhof"

Klaus Winter

Klaus Winter (May 29, 1936 in Essen - October 10, 2000) was a German judge. He was a judge in the Federal Constitutional Court of Germany.
Source (edited): "http://en.wikipedia.org/wiki/Klaus_Winter"

Konrad Hesse

Konrad Hesse (January 29, 1919 – March 15, 2005) was a German jurisprudence scientist and, from 1975 to 1987, judge at the Federal Constitutional Court of Germany.

Hesse was born in Königsberg, East Prussia. He entered the scientific field after his education in law. He obtained his doctorate degree in 1950, and was habilited in 1955 at the Georg-August University of Göttingen. His habilitation covered state, administration and canon laws. His first ordinary was received in 1965 at the Albert Ludwigs University of Freiburg. Additionally, he worked from 1961 to 1975 as a judge at the Supreme Administrative Court in Baden-Württemberg.

As a judge at the Federal Constitutional Court of Germany, Hesse was a member of the first senate and coined, in connection with the census judgement in 1983, the term of the right to informational self-determination. To solve the clash of civil rights, he produced the so-called term of practical concordance.

Since 2003 Hesse was a member of the Bavarian Academy of Sciences and Humanities. He died in Merzhausen.

Works and writings

- Grundzüge des Verfassungsrecht der Bundesrepublik Deutschland, 20. Auflage Heidelberg 1999, ISBN 3-8114-7499-5
- Verfassungsrecht und Privatrecht, Heidelberg 1988, ISBN 3-8114-8588-1

Source (edited): "http://en.wikipedia.org/wiki/Konrad_Hesse"

Lerke Osterloh

Lerke Osterloh (born September 29, 1944 in Wüsting-Holle near Oldenburg) is a German judge, jurisprudent and tax law expert. She was sitting Justice of the Federal Constitutional Court of Germany in the court's second senate from October 1998 until her retirement in November 2010. Her successor is Monika Hermanns. Along with Gertrude Lübbe-Wolff and Michael Gerhardt, she is considered a member of the senate's left-liberal wing.

Source (edited): "http://en.wikipedia.org/wiki/Lerke_Osterloh"

Michael Eichberger

Michael Eichberger is a German law scientist and a judge at the Federal Constitutional Court of Germany.

Life

Eichberger was born in Würzburg on June 23, 1953. Following his first state exam in law 1979 in Mannheim and his second one in 1981 in Baden-Württemberg he was a research assistant at the University of Mainz until 1984. Afterwards he did his doctoral dissertation there in 1985. Between 1984 and 1986 he was a judge at the administrative court in Karlsruhe. Later, from 1986 until 1989, he worked at the Justice Ministry of Baden-Württemberg. After that he worked at the Federal Constitutional Court of Germany as a research assistant until 1991. Since 1992 he was a judge at administrative court in Karlsruhe again and in 1993 he was delegated as a judge to the Higher Administrative Court of Baden-Württemberg in Mannheim, where he stayed until 1998. Since 1998/99 he was a docent at the University of Tübingen. Between 1998 and 2006 he was a judge at the Federal Administrative Court of Germany in Leipzig as well. 2004 he became an honorary professor at the University of Tübingen. In April 2006 he was appointed as a judge at the Federal Constitutional Court of Germany.

Source (edited): "http://en.wikipedia.org/wiki/Michael_Eichberger"

Paul Kirchhof

Paul Kirchhof (born February 21, 1943 in Osnabrück) is a German jurist and tax law expert. He is also a professor of law, member of the Pontifical Academy of Social Sciences and a former judge in the Federal Constitutional Court of Germany (*Bundesverfassungsgericht*), the highest court in Germany.

Kirchhof obtained a doctorate at the early age of 25 having studied law in Freiburg and Munich. He then became director of the Institute for Tax Law (*Institut für Steuerrecht*) at the University of Münster. In 1987 he was finally appointed to the Federal Constitutional Court of Germany in Karlsruhe, where he remained a judge until 1999. He then assumed the position of professor at the University of Heidelberg School of Law.

During the 2005 federal election campaign, Angela Merkel, leader of the CDU/CSU, announced that Kirchhof would serve as minister of finance if she formed a government. Kirchhof proposed to adopt a flat tax for Germany, with an income tax rate of 25% for nearly everybody. Chancellor Gerhard Schröder successfully mocked Kirchhof during the SPD's campaign, calling him "that professor from Heidelberg", implying Kirchhof an ivory-towered point of view.

This proposal undermined the CDU's credibility on economic affairs, and lead many Germans to believe that the party's platform for deregulation would only benefit the rich. It was a major contribution to the CDU's drop in the polls, from a lead of 21% over the SPD at the start of the election campaign to 9%. Merkel's own popularity dropped 10% when she publicly endorsed Kirchhof's flat tax proposals. Although Merkel's popularity improved after she later distanced herself from Kirchhof's proposals, the CDU has not recovered its earlier large lead in the polls. Kirchof attempted to bring the matter to a close before polling day by indicating that he would be remaining in academia and would not accept a position in government.

Kirchhof has very conservative opinions on issues such as family and feminism, although these did not become an issue during the campaign. He has been quoted as saying that "the mother's career lies in the family, which doesn't produce power, but friendship, not money, but happiness."

Kirchhof is the older brother of sitting Federal Constitutional Court Justice Ferdinand Kirchhof.
Source (edited): "http://en.wikipedia.org/wiki/Paul_Kirchhof"

Renate Jaeger

Renate Jaeger (30 December 1940 -) is a German lawyer and judge of the European Court of Human Rights. Her term at the Court expired on 30 December 2010.

Early life

Jaeger was born in Darmstadt, a city in the state of Hesse, Germany, and studied Law at Cologne, Munich and Lausanne. In 1968, after completing her legal training, she became a judge at the *Sozialgericht* of Düsseldorf in North Rhine-Westphalia. The *Sozialgericht* ('social court') is the lowest of three courts dealing with social security matters, the higher courts being the *Landessozialgericht* (state level) and national *Bundessozialgericht* (Federal Social Court of Germany).

Judicial career

Between 1970 and 1971, Jaeger was seconded as a research assistant to the *Bundessozialgericht*, and in 1974 was promoted to sit on the *Landessozialgericht* for North Rhine-Westphalia, remaining there until 1987. From 1976 to 1979, she was again seconded as a research assistant, this time to the *Bundesverfassungsgericht*, the Federal Constitutional Court of Germany. In 1986, she was promoted to Presiding Judge at the *Landessozialgericht*, and in 1987 was called to join the *Bundessozialgericht*.

As well as being a member of the Federal Social Court, Jaeger was appointed in 1988 to sit on the State Constitutional Court of North Rhein-Westphalia. From 1991 to 1994, she took on a lectureship at the University of Münster. On 24 March 1994, she was appointed a judge of the Federal Constitutional Court (*Bundesverfassungsgericht*) in the First Senate. She was also appointed Liaison Officer between the Court and the Council of Europe's Venice Commission.

On 28 April 2004, Jaeger was elected by the Parliamentary Assembly of the Council of Europe to be a judge on the European Court of Human Rights, based in Strasbourg, France, with effect from 1 November that year. On 14 October, she received an honorary doctorate by the University of Münster, and that Autumn was awarded the Grand Cross of the Order of Merit of the Federal Republic of Germany (*Großes Verdienstkreuz mit Stern und Schulterband*). She was succeeded at the Federal Constitutional Court by Reinhard Gaier. On 2 July 2009, she was elected Vice-President of one of the Court's Sections. Her term at the Court ended on 30 December 2010, and she was succeeded by Angelika Nussberger.

Charity

Jaeger is a member of the board of trustees of *Aktion Deutschland Hilft*, an alliance of German emergency aid organisations.
Source (edited): "http://en.wikipedia.org/wiki/Renate_Jaeger"

Roman Herzog

Roman Herzog (born 5 April 1934) is a German politician (CDU) and was President of Germany from 1994 to 1999. He was the first President of the Federal Republic of Germany to be elected to office after the reunification of Germany that took place in 1990, and the second person to serve as all-German head of State since the end of World War II.

Biography

Roman Herzog by Bertrand Freiesleben 2008

Roman Herzog was born in Landshut, Bavaria in 1934 to a Protestant family.

He studied law in Munich and took his first juristic state exam in 1957. In 1958, he gained the title *Doctor juris* and worked as an assistant at the University of Munich until 1964, where he also passed his second juristic state exam. For his paper *Die Wesensmerkmale der Staatsorganisation in rechtlicher und entwicklungsgeschichtlicher Sicht* ("Characteristics of State Organization from a Juristic and Developmental-Historical Viewpoint"), in 1964 he was awarded the title of professor, a title of academic distinction in Germany, and taught at the University of Munich until 1966. From 1966 he taught state law and political science as a full professor at the Free University of Berlin (FUB). In 1969 he accepted an administrative position at the FUB in Speyer, and was the University President from 1971 to 1972.

In 1973 his political career began as a representative of the state (*Land*) of Rhineland-Palatinate with the Federal government in Bonn. He was minister for culture and sports in the Baden-Württemberg State Government from 1978. In 1980 he was elected to the State Parliament (*Landtag*), and took over the state Ministry of the Interior.

Roman Herzog has also always been active in the Evangelical Church in Germany. Until 1980 he was head of the Chamber for public responsibility of this church and since 1982 he has been a member of the synod of the Evangelical Church in Germany.

In 1983 he became a judge at the Federal Constitutional Court of Germany ("*Bundesverfassungsgericht*") in Karlsruhe. From 1987 until 1994, he also served as the president of this Court, until he was elected President of Germany by the Federal Assembly (Bundesversammlung) in 1994. He retained this position until 1999, when he was succeeded by Johannes Rau.

In 1994 Herzog participated in the commemorations of the 50th anniversary of the Warsaw Uprising during the Nazi occupation of Poland. In a widely commended speech he paid tribute to the Polish fighters and people and asked Poles for "forgiveness for what has been done to you by the Germans".

Between December 1999 and October 2000, he was chair of the European Convention which drafted the Charter of Fundamental Rights of the European Union.

His wife, Christiane Herzog, died on 19 June 2000. He later married Alexandra Freifrau von Berlichingen.

Source (edited): "http://en.wikipedia.org/wiki/Roman_Herzog"

Rudolf Katz

Rudolf Katz (23 November 1895 – 23 July 1961) was a German politician and judge. He was Vice President of the Federal Constitutional Court of Germany.

Biography

Katz was born in Falkenburg, Farther Pomerania (modern Złocieniec, Poland) to Leopold Katz, a teacher and Jewish Kantor, and Hulda Katz. The family moved to Kiel in 1897, where Katz grew up. He began to study law at the University of Kiel in 1913 but volunteered for the German Army in World War I. Katz served as a Lieutenant and was wounded several times, he finished his studies in 1919 and gained his doctorate in 1920.

Katz joined the Social Democratic Party of Germany in 1920 and the Reichsbanner Schwarz-Rot-Gold in 1924. Katz was elected a member of the city council of Altona in 1929 and became its chairman in 1932. He worked as a lawyer (1924–33) and notary (1929–33) in Altona. In 1930 he left the Jewish Parish. Katz pleaded for communist defendants in the aftermath of the Altona Bloody Sunday of July 1932.

After Hitler took over power in Germany Katz fled to France in March 1933. Along with Max Brauer, a Social Democrat and mayor of Altona, Katz became an envoy for municipal administration of the League of Nations in Nanjing in October 1933. In 1935 he moved to the United States and worked at the Columbia University's Institute for Public Administration and as a journalist for the Neue Volkszeitung, a German-language newspaper of socialdemocrat emigrants. Katz was a director of the Rand School of Social Science in New York and of The New Leader newspaper, he was active in the German Labour Delegation, part of the American Federation of Labor, and the *"German-American Council for the Liberation of Germany from Nazism"*.

After Katz had lost his German citizenship because of the racialist Nazi laws, he became an United States citizen in 1941.

In July 1946 Katz returned to Germany along with Max Brauer and became Minister of Justice (1947–50) and Education (1948–49) in the State of Schleswig-Holstein. He regained his German citizenship in November 1947 and represented Schleswig-Holstein in the Parlamentarischer Rat, ("Parliamentary Council"), the predecessor of the West German Bundestag. In the negotiations of the German constitution Katz successfully proposed the invention of the Constructive vote of no confidence, while his suggestion to limit the number of members of the Bundestag to 300 and to implement a minimum threshold of 10 percent of votes failed.

In 1951 Katz became the Chairman of the secondnd Senate and Vice President of the Federal Constitutional Court of Germany. He was elected a member of the executive board of the International Commission of Jurists at the New Delhi Congress in 1959.

Katz was married to Agnes Kühl in 1933. He died in Baden-Baden.
Source (edited): "http://en.wikipedia.org/wiki/Rudolf_Katz"

Rudolf Mellinghoff

Rudolf Mellinghoff (born November 25, 1954) is a German judge, jurisprudent and tax law expert. Since January, 2001, he is sitting Justice of the Federal Constitutional Court of Germany in the court's second senate. Prior to his appointment to the court, he has served as judge in the Federal Finance Court of Germany from 1997 to 2001.
Source (edited): "http://en.wikipedia.org/wiki/Rudolf_Mellinghoff"

Susanne Baer

Susanne Baer in November 2010

Susanne Baer (* 1964) is a German legal scholar and a judge of the Federal Constitutional Court of Germany.

Life

Baer was born in Saarbrücken on February 16, 1964. From 1983 to 1988 Baer studied German law and Political science at Free University of Berlin. From 2002 to 2011 Baer was legal scholar at Humboldt University of Berlin in Berlin. Since February 2011 Baer is a judge of the Federal Constitutional Court. She is after judge Brun-Otto Bryde the second judge of the Federal Constitutional Court to be elected on the proposal of the Green party. Baer lives in a civil union.

Works

- *Comparative Constitutionalism: Cases and Materials*, (together with Norman Dorsen, Michel Rosenfeld, András Sajó), St. Paul 2010

Source (edited): "http://en.wikipedia.org/wiki/Susanne_Baer"

Udo Di Fabio

Udo Di Fabio (born March 26, 1954 in Duisburg) is a German jurist and a member of the Federal Constitutional Court of Germany, Germany's highest court.
Source (edited): "http://en.wikipedia.org/wiki/Udo_Di_Fabio"

Udo Steiner

Udo Steiner (born September 16, 1939 in Bayreuth) was a Judge at the Federal Constitutional Court of Germany from 1995 to 2007.

He grew up in Franconia, and went on to study law in Erlangen, Saarbrücken and Cologne. In 1965, he earned a doctorate with the thesis *Verfassunggebung und verfassunggebende Gewalt des Volkes*. Subsequently, he earned his Habilitation in 1972, with the thesis *Öffentliche Verwaltung durch Private*.

In 1973, Steiner was appointed as Professor of Public Law at the University of Erlangen, and subsequently served as Professor at the universities of Göttingen, Bielefeld and Regensburg. He was Dean of the Faculty of Law at the University of Bielefeld from 1976 to 1977, and in Regensburg from 1988 to 1990. Between 1976 and 1979, he also served as a Judge at the Oberverwaltungsgericht.

He was appointed a Judge at the Federal Constitutional Court in October 1995, and still lectures at the University of Regensburg. He was retired as a Judge upon turning 68 in 2007, and was succeeded by Ferdinand Kirchhof.

In 2008, he was appointed as the Ombudsman of Deutsche Bahn for victims of railway accidents.

Steiner married in 1967 and has four children.

Honours

- 2007: Großes Verdienstkreuz mit Stern und Schulterband
- 2008: Bayerischer Verdienstorden

Source (edited): "http://en.wikipedia.org/wiki/Udo_Steiner"

Walter Rudi Wand

Walter Rudi Wand (September 7, 1928 – June 29, 1985) was a German judge and bureaucrat. He was a judge in the Federal Constitutional Court of Germany.
Source (edited): "http://en.wikipedia.org/wiki/Walter_Rudi_Wand"

Willi Geiger (judge)

Geiger in 1951

Willi Geiger (May 22, 1909 in Neustadt an der Weinstraße - January 19, 1994 in Karlsruhe) was a German judge. He was a judge in the Federal Constitutional Court of Germany
Source (edited): "http://en.wikipedia.org/wiki/Willi_Geiger_(judge)"

Winfried Hassemer

Winfried Hassemer (born 17 February 1940), is a German criminal law scholar. He was vice-president of the Federal Constitutional Court.

Born in Gau-Algesheim, Hassemer was from 1964–1969 a scientific assistant at the Institut for laws and social philosophy of the university of Saarland. He is married with Kristiane Weber Hassemer, the chairmen judge of a criminal senate at the higher regional court of Frankfurt/Main and chairmen of national ethics advice of Germany. His brother Volker Hassemer was a senator in Berlin.
Source (edited): "http://en.wikipedia.org/wiki/Winfried_Hassemer"

Wolfgang Zeidler

Wolfgang Zeidler (September 2, 1924 – December 31, 1987) was a German legal scholar and judge. He served as the

East Prussian plebiscite

1920 map of Poland and the Baltic States showing area of the East Prussian plebiscite.

The **East Prussia(n) plebiscite** (German: *Abstimmung in Ostpreußen*), also known as the **Allenstein and Marienwerder plebiscite** or **Warmia, Masuria and Powiśle plebiscite** (Polish: *Plebiscyt na Warmii, Mazurach i Powiślu*), was a plebiscite for self-determination of the regions Warmia (Ermland), Masuria (Mazury, Masuren) and Powiśle, which had been in parts of East Prussia and West Prussia, in accordance with Articles 94 to 97 of the Treaty of Versailles. Prepared during early 1920, it took place on 11 July 1920. The majority of voters selected East Prussia over Poland (over 97% in Allenstein (Olsztyn) and 92% in Marienwerder (Kwidzyn)); most of the territories in question thus remained in the Free State of Prussia, and therefore, in Germany.

Historical background

The districts concerned had changed hands at various times over the centuries between Old Prussians, Monastic state of the Teutonic Knights, Germany, and Poland. The area of Warmia was part of the Kingdom of Prussia since the first partition of Poland in 1772 and the region of Masuria was ruled by the German Hohenzollern family since the Prussian Tribute of 1525 (as a Polish fief till 1660). Many inhabitants of that region had Polish roots and were influenced by Polish culture; the last official German census in 1910 classified them as Poles or Masurians. The Polish delegation at the Paris Peace Conference, led by Roman Dmowski, made a number of demands in relation to those areas which were part of the Polish-Lithuanian Commonwealth until 1772 and despite their protests, supported by the French, President Woodrow Wilson and the other allies agreed that plebiscites should be held.

Regions of the plebiscite

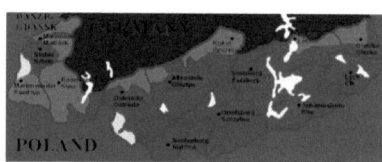

A Polish map showing languages of Mazury and Warmia in 1920s. Red: Second Polish Republic. Blue: Germany. Yellow: territories incorporated into Poland as a result of the plebiscite. Green: territories with a majority of speakers of the Polish language (or Masurian dialect of Polish). Grey: territories with a majority of speakers of the German language. Brown: borders of *landkreis*.

Plebiscite results, black sections of the piecharts show the Polish share of votes

The plebiscite areas were placed under the authority of two Inter-Allied Commissions of five members appointed by the Principal Allied and Associated Powers representing the League of Nations. British and Italian troops under the command of these Commissions had arrived on and soon after February 12, 1920. The regular German Reichswehr had previously left the area. Civil and municipal administration was continued under the existing German authorities who were responsible to the Commissions for their duration.

In accordance with Articles 94 to 97 of the Treaty of Versailles (section entitled "East Prussia") the territory of the plebiscite was formed by Marienwerder (Kwidzyn) district (*Landkreis Marienwerder* - Marienwerder district) which encompassed counties of Stuhm (Sztum), Rosenberg in Westpreußen (Susz) as well as parts of counties of Marienburg (Malbork) east off the Nogat river) and Marienwerder (east of the Vistula river). The treaty defined the area as "The western and northern boundary of Regierungsbezirk Allenstein (Allenstein district) to its junction with the boundary between the Kreise (district) of Oletzko (Olecko) and Angerburg (Węgorzewo); thence, the northern boundary of the Kreis of Oletzko to its junction with the old frontier of East Prussia."

H. D. Beaumont, the British representative on the Marienwerder Plebiscite Commission, reported to Earl Curzon on February 25, 1920, that the total population of his Plebiscite Area was approximately 158,300, of whom 134,500 were claimed to be of German race and 23,800 Poles, or 15%.

Allenstein (Olsztyn) region

Handover of the Plebiscite area by the Allied commission, Allenstein 16 August 1920

The President of and British Commissioner on the Inter-Allied Administrative and Plebiscite Commission for Allenstein was Mr. Ernest Rennie; French Commissioner was M. Couget; the Marquis Fracassi, a Senator, for Italy; Mr. Marumo for Japan. The German Government were permitted under the Protocol terms to attach a delegate and they sent Baron von Gayl, formerly in the service of the Interior Ministry and lately on the Colonization Committee. The local police forces were placed under the control of two British officers, Lieutenant-Colonel Bennet and Major David Deevis. Bennet reported that he regarded them as "well-disciplined and reliable". There was also present a battalion from the Royal Irish Regiment and an Italian regiment stationed at Lyck (Ełk).

This Commission had general powers of administration and, in particular, was "charged with the duty of arranging for the vote and of taking such measures as it may deem necessary to ensure its freedom, fairness, and secrecy. The Commission will have all necessary authority to decide any questions to which the execution of these provisions may give rise. The Commission will make such arrangements as may be necessary for assistance in the exercise of its functions by officials chosen by itself from the local population. Its decisions will be taken by a majority."

Marienwerder (Kwidzyn) region

Beaumont and the other members of the Commission reached Marienwerder on February 17, 1920. Upon their arrival they found an Italian battalion of Bersaglieri on guard who afterwards marched past at the double. This commission had about 1,400 uniformed German police under its authority.

The difficulties

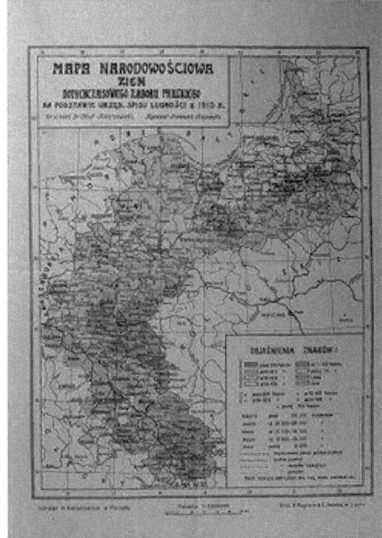

A Polish map 1910.

5-Pfennig stamp. To advertise the plebiscite, special postage stamps were produced by overprinting German stamps and sold from 3 April. One kind of overprint read **PLÉBISCITE / OLSZTYN / ALLENSTEIN**, while the other read **TRAITÉ / DE / VERSAILLES / ART. 94 et 95** inside an oval whose border gave the full name of the plebiscite commission. Each overprint was applied to 14 denominations ranging from 5 Pf to 3 M.

Beaumont said that with the exception of the Kreis of Stuhm (Sztum), where Poles admittedly numbered 15,500 out of a population of 36,500 (42%), the German sympathies of the inhabitants were clearly evident. He added that "immense sums have been spent in the past on railways, roads, bridges and public buildings." Beaumont continued: "the frontier is strictly guarded by the Poles with people having business on the other side prevented from passing without having to go through vexatious formalities. Trains are deliberately held up for hours on entering and leaving Polish territory or the service suspended altogether. Postal, telegraphic and telephonic communication is constantly interrupted. To pass into the territory of the Free City of Danzig it is necessary to cross through a narrow strip of Polish territory by the great bridge over the Vistula at Dirschau [Tczew]. Here the way is barred by sentries (in French uniforms) who refuse to understand any language but Polish, and a similar barrier has been established at the little village of Muhlhaus before again entering Danzig territory. The result is that this area is cut off from its shopping centre and chief port almost completely. Although it is scarcely likely to change the result of the Plebiscite it would in my opinion be desirable to convey a hint to the Warsaw Government that their present policy is scarcely calculated to gain them votes."

Sir Horace Rumbold, the British Minister in Warsaw, also wrote to Curzon on March 5, 1920, saying that the Plebiscite Commissions at Allenstein and Marienwerder "felt that they were isolated both from Poland and from Germany" and that the Polish authorities were holding up supplies of coal and petrol to those districts. Sir Horace had a meeting with the Polish Minister for Foreign Affairs, M. Patek, who declared he was disappointed with his people's behaviour and "spoke strongly about the tactlessness and rigidity of the Polish Military authorities."

On March 10, 1920, Beaumont wrote of numerous continuing difficulties being made by Polish officials and added "as a result, the ill-will between Polish and German nationalities and the irritation due to Polish intolerance towards the German inhabitants in the Corridor (now under their rule), far worse than any former German intolerance of the Poles, are growing to such an extent that it is impossible to believe the present settlement (borders) can have any chance of being permanent.... It can confidently be asserted that not even the most attractive economic advantages would induce any German to vote Polish. If the frontier is unsatisfactory now it will be far more so when it has to be drawn on this side (of the river) with no natural line to follow, cutting off Germany from the river bank and within a mile or so of Marienwerder, which is certain to vote German. I know of no similar frontier created by any treaty."

The Poles began to harden their position and Rumbold reported to Curzon on March 22, 1920 that Count Przezdziecki, an official of the Polish Foreign Office, had told Sir Percy Loraine (1st Secretary in H.M. Legation at Warsaw) that the Poles questioned the impartiality of the Inter-Allied Commissions and indicated that the Polish Government might refuse to recognise the results of the Plebiscites.

Propaganda

The "German House", the headquarter of the *Ostdeutsche Heimatdienst* in Allenstein in July 1920

Both sides started a propaganda campaign. Already in March 1919 Paul Hensel, the Lutheran Superintendent of Johannisburg, travelled to Versailles to hand over a collection of 144,447 signatures to the Allied Powers to protest against the planned cession. The Germans founded several regional associations under the title of the "Ostdeutsche Heimatdienst", which had above 220,000 members. They put their emphasis on Prussian history and loyalty to the Prussian state and also used prejudices against Polish culture and Poland's economical backwardness. Rennie, the British Commissioner in Allenstein, reported on March 11, 1920, that "in those parts which touch the Polish frontier a vigorous German propaganda is in progress", and that "the Commission is doing all it can to prevent German officials in the district from taking part in national propaganda in connection with the Plebiscite. Ordnances and instructions in this sense have been issued."

Rennie reported to Curzon at the British Foreign Office, on February 18, 1920, that the Poles, who had taken control of the Polish Corridor to the Baltic Sea, had "entirely disrupted the railway, telegraphic and telephone system, and the greatest difficulty is being experienced. Colonel Lomas, the head of the Communications Department, has left for Warsaw to negotiate with the Polish Authorities and to endeavour to remedy matters."

Rennie reported on March 11, 1920, that the Polish Consul-General, Dr. Lewandowski, aged about 60 and a former chemist who kept a shop in Poznań (Posen), had arrived. Rennie states: "he apparently has little experience of official life, and immediately after his arrival he began sending to the Commission complaints, frequently couched in extravagant language, declaring that the entire Polish population of this district have been terrorised for years and are as a result unable to or incapable of expressing their sentiments. I have to say Dr. Lewandowski's attitude is not always judicious as may be instanced by the incident which occurred on Sunday last in connection with the hoisting of the Polish flag over the consular office. Dr. Lewandowski had been recognised only four days previously, and, without giving notice of his intention to the Commission, proceeded to hoist his flag from his office window, which is situated in the same building and alongside the office of the Polish Propaganda Department. On seeing this the population, perhaps not unnaturally, showed its resentment. The police had to be summoned, entered the building, and removed the flag. However, at 4 o'clock in the afternoon the flag was again flown and the police had to be posted outside the building to prevent trouble and the flag was hauled down at 5 p.m. I pointed out to Dr. Lewandowski that he ought to realise that his position here was a delicate one........and I added it was highly desirable that his office should not be situated in a building with the Bureau of Polish propaganda."

Undercover and illicit activities were also commenced and as early as March 11, 1920 the Earl of Derby reported a decision of the Allied Council of Ambassadors in Paris to make representations to the Polish government regarding violations of the frontiers of the Marienwerder district by Polish soldiers.

Beaumont reported from Marienwerder at the end of March that "no change has been made in the methods of Polish propaganda. Occasional meetings are held, but they are attended only by Poles in small numbers." He continues "acts and articles violently abusive of everything German in the newly founded Polish newspaper appear to be the only (peaceful) methods adopted to persuade the inhabitants of the Plebiscite areas to vote for Poland."

The Poles established an unofficial Masurian Plebiscite Committee (Mazurski Komitet Plebiscytowy) on June 6, 1919 under the chairmanship of Juliusz Bursche, later Bishop of the Evangelical-Augsburg Church in Poland. There was also an unofficial Warmian Plebiscite Committee (Warmiński Komitet Plebiscytowy). They argued that the Masurians of Warmia and Masuria were victims of a long period of Germanization, but ethnic Poles, now had the opportunity to liberate themselves from Prussian rule.

After the vote, the Poles felt disadvantaged by the Versailles Treaty stipulation which enabled those who were born in the plebiscite area but not living there any more to return to vote. Approximately 152,000 such individuals participated in the plebiscite. There is confusion on whether this was a Polish or German condition at Versailles as it might have been expected that many Ruhrpolen would vote for Poland,. While it is reported, that the Polish delegation planned to bring Polish émigrés not only from other parts of Germany but also from America to the plebiscite area to strengthen their position, the Polish delegation claimed that it was a German condition.

The plebiscite

The plebiscites asked the voters whether they wanted their homeland to remain in East Prussia, which was part of Weimar Germany, or instead become part of Poland (the alternatives for the voters were not Germany / Poland, but East Prussia / Poland). All inhabitants of the plebiscite district older than 20 years of age or those who were born in this area before 1 January 1905, were entitled to return to vote.

The plebiscite took place on 11 July 1920; at the time Poland appeared on the verge of defeat in the Polish-Soviet War (see Miracle at the Vistula). German Prussia was able to organize a very successful propaganda campaign, building on the long campaign of Germanization; notably the plebiscite masked the German choice under the regional name of Prussia. The activity of German organizations, and the Allied support for the participation of Masurians who were born in Masuria but did not live there any longer, further aided the German cause. Hence the plebiscite ended with a majority of the voters voting for Prussia, only a small part of the territory affected by the plebiscite was awarded to Poland, with the majority going to Germany.

Results

Results as published by Poland thus with Polish name first.

Olsztyn/Allenstein

The results for Olsztyn/Allenstein region were:
registered voters: 425,305, valid: 371,189, turnout: 87.31%

To honour the exceptionally high percentage of pro-German votes in the district of Oletzko (de:Landkreis Oletzko), with 2 votes for Poland compared to 28,625 for Germany, the main town Marggrabowa (Margrave town) was renamed "*Treuburg*" (Treue = "faithfulness") in 1928, with the district following this example in 1933.

In the villages of Lubstynek (Klein Lobenstein), Czerlin (Klein Nappern) and Groszki (Groschken) in the Kreis Osterode/district of Osterode (Ostróda), situated directly at the border, a majority voted for Poland. These villages became a part of Poland after the plebiscite.

Due to the Prussian Eastern Railway line Danzig-Warsaw passing there, the area of Soldau in Landkreis Neidenburg was transferred to Poland without plebiscite, and renamed Działdowo.

Marienwerder / Kwidzyn

The results for Kwidzyn/Marienwerder region were:
registered voters: 125,090 valid: 104,941 turnout: 84.00%

The plebiscite district remained with German East Prussia as the Regierungsbezirk Westpreussen.
Source (edited): "http://en.wikipedia.org/wiki/East_Prussian_plebiscite"

German election and referendum, 1936

The third Nazi plebiscite, this German referendum was held on 29 March 1936. The purpose of the referendum was to obtain public support for the military occupation of the Rhineland and approve of a single party list composed exclusively by Nazi (as well as formally independent "guest") candidates for the new Reichstag. Like previous elections in Nazi Germany, it was characterized by high turnout, voter intimidation and a massively one-sided result, with an official 99.0% turnout. In a publicity stunt, a handful of voters were packed aboard the airships Graf Zeppelin and Hindenburg, which flew above the Rhineland as those aboard cast their ballots.

The new Reichstag convened for formulary procedures on 30 January 1937 to re-elect its Presidium and Hermann Göring as President of the Reichstag.
Source (edited): "http://en.wikipedia.org/wiki/German_election_and_referendum,_1936"

German election and referendum, 1938

The final elections to the German Reichstag during Nazi rule referendum, held on 10 April 1938, asked German and Austrian voters to approve of a single Nazi-party list for the new 814 member German Reichstag as well as Adolf Hitler's recent annexation of Austria, the *Anschluss*. Turnout in the general election was officially 99.6% with 99.1% voting "yes". In the case of Austria, Hitler's native soil, 99.71% of an electorate of 4,484,475 officially went to the ballots, with a positive tally of 99.73%.

The election for Reichstag was the last on a national scale during Nazi rule and was held largely to rally official support from the new *Ostmark* (Austrian) province, although another rubber-stamp election was held in the recently-annexed Sudetenland on 4 December. In this last election under Nazi rule, the NSDAP candidates (including non-member "guests") officially tallied 97.32% of the votes.

The new Reichstag, the last of the German Reich, convened for the first time on 30 January 1939, electing a presidium headed by incumbent President of the Reichstag Hermann Göring. It convened only a further seven times, the last on 26 July 1942.

In 25 January 1943, the Führer postponed elections for a new Reichstag until "after" the war, with the inaugural to take place after another electoral term, subsequently on 30 January 1947 (at which point the body had ceased to exist).

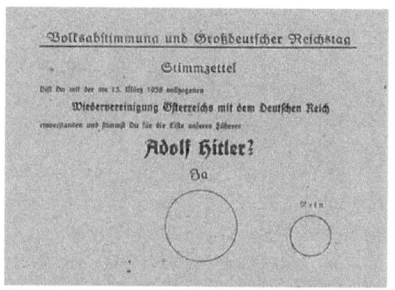

Voting card, text reading: "*Do you approve of the reunification of Austria with the German reich accomplished on 13 March 1938 and do you vote for the list of our Führer, Adolf Hitler?*" The voter would simply cross a *yes* or *no* to show favor in both issues or not.

Source (edited): "http://en.wikipedia.org/wiki/German_election_and_referendum,_1938"

German referendum, 1933

Held on the same day as the November 1933 Elections, the referendum was designed to gauge public approval and support for Hitler's decision to withdraw Nazi Germany from the League of Nations and the World Disarmament Conference.

Source (edited): "http://en.wikipedia.org/wiki/German_referendum,_1933"

German referendum, 1934

Held on August 19, 1934, after the death of President Paul von Hindenburg seventeen days earlier, the German leadership sought to gain approval for Adolf Hitler's assumption of supreme leadership. The overwhelmingly positive result of this referendum allowed Hitler to claim public support for his activities as the Führer and *de facto* Head of State of Germany. In fact, he had assumed these offices and powers immediately upon von Hindenburg's death and used the referendum to legitimate this move, taking the title *Führer und Reichskanzler* (Führer and Chancellor).

Source (edited): "http://en.wikipedia.org/wiki/German_referendum,_1934"

Schleswig Plebiscites

Map of Schleswig / South Jutland before the plebiscites.

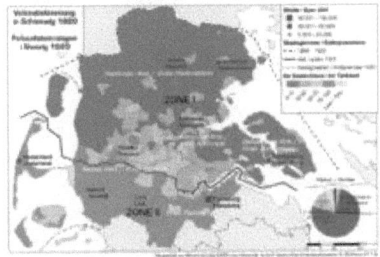

Results of the plebiscite.

The **Schleswig Plebiscites** were two plebiscites, organized according to section XII, articles 109 to 114 of the Treaty of Versailles of June 28, 1919, in order to determine the future border between Denmark and Germany through the former duchy of Schleswig. The process was monitored by a commission with representatives from France, the United Kingdom, Norway and Sweden.

The Danish-ruled Duchy of Schleswig had been conquered by Prussia and Austria in the 1864 Second War of Schleswig along with the Danish-ruled German provinces of Holstein and Lauenburg. Article 5 of the Austro-Prussian Peace of Prague stipulated that a plebiscite should be held within 6 years to give the people of the northern part of Schleswig the possibility of voting between staying German or separating parts of Schleswig and repartitioning them to Denmark, an arrangement already denied by Denmark after the war of 1848 and again after the war of 1864, and then dropped completely in 1878 in the Treaty of Gastein between Austria and Imperial Germany. The border was respected later by both Denmark and Germany in the Optant Treaty of Copenhagen 1907. After the defeat of Germany in World War I Germany was forced to accept a plebiscite whose unilateral conditions then were defined by Denmark.

The plebiscites were held in two zones that were defined by Denmark. according to the ideas of the Danish historian Hans Victor Clausen Zone I was dimensioned as far towards the South as possible, therefore changing the Clausen-Line southerly from Tondern instead of northerly, and had to vote *en bloc*, i.e. as a unit with the majority deciding, while in the following smaller Zone II each municipality was to decide its own allegiance, this procedure allowing Denmark to gain further territory and put the frontier further southwards according to eventual majorities in northern municipalities.

The first plebiscite was held in *Zone I*, the later Northern Schleswig on February 10, 1920. 74.9 % (75,431 votes) of the public voted to come under Danish rule, 25.1 % (25,329 votes) to stay German, although in three of the four major towns and especially in the southern region directly at the frontier to Zone II German majorities existed, especially a large German majority between 70 and 80 percent in and around Tønder and Højer. It was mostly this area that caused discussions after the voting, especially as this area had been regarded also by Clausen to be south of an imaginary German-Danish border.

Central Schleswig (*Zone II*) voted on March 14, 1920. 80.2 % (51,742 votes) fell to Germany, 19.8 % (12,800) to Denmark. Since a Danish majority in this zone was only produced in three small villages on the island of Föhr not aligned with the coming border, the *Commission Internationale de Surveillance du Plébiscite Slésvig* decided on a line almost completely identical to the border between the two zones. The poor result for Denmark in Central Schleswig - particularly in Flensburg, Schleswig's largest city - triggered Denmark's 1920 Easter Crisis.

A plebiscite was not held in the southernmost third of the province (*Zone III*) as there was no doubt about the outcome.

Selected results in detail:

Zone I (Northern Schleswig):
- **District Haderslehen / Haderslev**: 16.0 % (6,585 votes) Germany, 84.0 % (34,653 votes) Denmark, thereof
  - Town of Haderslehen / Haderslev: 38.6 % (3,275 votes) Germany, 61.4 % (5,209 votes) Denmark;
- **District Apenrade / Aabenraa: 32.3 % (6,030 votes) Germany, 67.7 % (12,653 votes) Denmark, thereof**
  - Town Apenrade / Aabenraa: 55.1 % (2,725 votes) Germany, 44.9 % (2,224 votes) Denmark;
- **District Sonderburg / Sønderborg**: 22.9 % (5,083 votes) Germany, 77.1 % (17,100 votes) Denmark, thereof
  - Town Sonderburg / Sønderborg: 56.2 % (2,601 votes) Germany, 43.8 % (2,029 votes) Denmark and
  - Spot Augustenburg / Augustenborg: 48.0 % (236 votes) Germany, 52.0 % (votes) Denmark;
- **District Tondern / Tønder, northern part**: 40.9 % (7,083 votes) Germany, 59.1 % (10,223 votes) Denmark, thereof
  - Town of Tondern / Tønder: 76.5 % (2,448 votes) Germany, 23.5 % (750 votes) Denmark,
  - Spot Hoyer / Højer: 72.6 % (581 votes) Germany, 27.4 % (219 votes) Denmark and
  - Spot Lügumkloster / Løgumkloster: 48.8 % (516

votes) Germany, 51.2 % (542 votes) Denmark;
- **District Flensburg / Flensborg, northern part**: 40.6 % (548 votes) Germany, 59.4 % (802 votes) Denmark.

Zone II (Central Schleswig):
- **District Tondern / Tønder, southern part**: 87.9 % (17,283 votes) Germany, 12.1 % (2,376 votes) Denmark;
- **District Flensburg / Flensborg, southern part**: 82.6 % (6,688 votes) Germany, 17.4 % (1,405 votes) Denmark;
- **District Husum, northern part**: 90.0 % (672 votes) Germany, 10.0 % (75 votes) Denmark;
- **Town of Flensburg / Flensborg**: 75.2 % (27,081 votes) Germany, 24.8 % (8,944 votes) Denmark.

Directly after the announcement of the results from Zone I, an alternative draft for the frontier was made by the German historian Johannes Tiedje. The proposed frontier would have incorporated Tondern, Hoyer, Tingleff and neighbouring areas and also some parts northern from Flensburg – the so called Tiedje Belt – and would have created almost equal minorities on both sides of the frontier instead of 30,000 to 35,000 Germans in Denmark and 6,000 to 8,000 Danes in Germany.

This and suggestions like this were not accepted and so Northern Schleswig was surrendered to Denmark on 15 June 1920, and the territory was officially named the *South Jutlandic districts*, more commonly Southern Jutland, although this name is historically identical to the whole of Schleswig.

Source (edited): "http://en.wikipedia.org/wiki/Schleswig_Plebiscites"

Constitution of Hamburg

The **Constitution of the Free and Hanseatic city of Hamburg** (German: *Verfassung der Freien und Hansestadt Hamburg*) is the basic governing document of the German city-state of Hamburg. It was approved on 6 June 1952. It is the fourth constitution that the state has had, consists of 76 articles and has been amended 13 times.

History

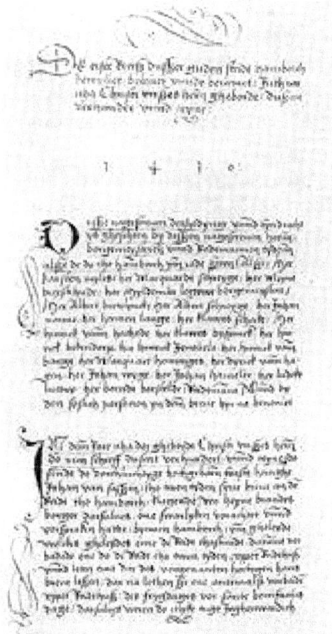

The first *Rezeß* of 1410.

Erich and Martin Verg considered a document called "the first Rezeß" of 1410 as the first constitution of Hamburg, although it has had no democratically founded proceedings to establish it.

The first constitution was established on 28 September 1860. It introduced a form of a representative democracy but with a limited right to vote, e.g. only male could vote. On 13 October 1879 a new constitution (*Verfassung der freien und Hansestadt Hamburg*) was created.

After the First World War in 1919 in the parliamentary Weimar Republic, the Hamburg Parliament ratified a temporary constitution (*Gesetz über die Vorläufige Staatsgewalt*) and a constitution (*Verfassung der Freien und Hansestadt Hamburg*) was formally approved in 1921.

The constitution of 1952 was ratified by the Hamburg Parliament.

Content

The constitution consists of 76 articles and a preamble. Dieter Läpple described the important connection between the port and the trade city to enter it into the preamble of the constitution as follows: *The preamble of the constitution of Hamburg points out the close relationship between port and city with regard to their development: „As an international port the Free and Hanseatic City of Hamburg has a special task, allocated by its history and location, to perform for the German people. In the spirit of peace it wants to be an intermediary between all continents and peoples of the world."*

It is divided into the following sections:
- legal foundations (I). In contrary to the other two city-states Berlin and Bremen the constitution does not separate between state (Land) and local communal affairs.
- sections for the Hamburg Parliament (II) and senate (III)
- law (IV) and adminsitration (V)
- jurisdiction (VI)
- budget and finance (VII)
- and final and transitional provisions (VIII)

Because the constitution was approved in 1959, after the Basic Law for the Federal Republic of Germany (approved in 1949) — which is the document that establishes and describes the duties, powers, structure and function of the government in Germany and legal also for the German states (*federal law breaking state law*) — a part for the human or basic rights (fundamental rights) is missing.

Constitutional institutions

The legislature is the Hamburg Parliament, for the judiciary there is the Hamburg Constitutional Court (*Hamburgisches Verfassungsgericht*) and the executive is represented by the senate (the cabinet), with its head the First Mayor of Hamburg (*Erster Bürgermeister der Freien und Hansestadt Hamburg*) equivalent to a prime minister or minister-president.

Amendments
The constitution has been amended 13 times since 1952.
Source (edited): "http://en.wikipedia.org/wiki/Constitution_of_Hamburg"

Constitution of Hesse

The **Constitution of Hesse**, signed on the December 1, 1946, is the constitution for the German state of Hesse.

Origins
A committee was formed for the preparation of the draft constitution and made up of 12 participants from each party. Participants of the advisory state committee (German:Beratenden Landesausschusses) February 26 - July 14, 1946 were, among others, Walter Fisch and Eleonore Wolf.

On June 30, 1946 elections were held for the state constitutional convention (Ger:verfassungsberatenden Landesversammlung). Out of a total election turnout of 71%, the Social Democratic Party (SPD) got 44.3% of the delegates, the Christian Democratic Union (CDU) 37.3%, the Communist Party (KPD) 9.7% and the Liberal Democratic Party (LDP) got 6%.

There were 51 participants at the state constitutional convention July 15 - November 30, 1946. (List:)

Other people involved in the development of the Hesse Constitution:
- Dr. Valentin Heckert. Drafted as assistant secretary of state (Ger.: Ministerialdirektor) for the production of a draft of the new constitution. He got involved with, among other things, the democratization of the police.
- Oskar Müller, Labor Secretary (Ger. Arbeitsminister) of the first Hesse government.
- Emil Carlebach, delegate of the first parliament and publisher of the German daily, Frankfurter Rundschau.

The state convention adopted the historic Hesse Constitutional Compromise on September 30, 1946. On December 1, 1946, the Hesse Constitution took effect by popular vote as the first German postwar constitution, with 76.4% for the entire constitution and 72% for socialization article 41.

Article 41 provided for socialization in the mining, iron and steel sectors, as well as in energy and transportation.

Other points of constitutional importance were recognition of the dignity and humanity of people; in the economic sphere, this included the right to work, the eight-hour workday, minimum 12 days of vacation, the right to strike, as well as a uniform industrial law for workers, employees and officials in which lockout is prohibited. Due of the recency of historical events under Naziism, the social aspects of the constitution went much further than they did in constitutions adopted later on by the other Federal states in Germany.

Article 21 remains a legal curiosity. According to it, the death penalty may be imposed for particularly grave crimes. Although the pertinent passage has not been struck from the constitution even to the present day, it is no longer in effect due to the abolishment of the death penalty at the level of the Federal constitution. The same goes for lockout, which is unlawful according to the Hesse constitution.
Source (edited): "http://en.wikipedia.org/wiki/Constitution_of_Hesse"

Constitution of North Rhine-Westphalia

The **Constitution of North Rhine-Westphalia** (German: *Verfassung für das Land Nordrhein-Westfalen*) in the constitutional document that governs the responsibilities and rights of various offices and the Landtag (State Parliament) of North Rhine-Westphalia, in Germany.

Background
After the collapse of the Third Reich after the Second World War, the area now covered by North Rhine-Westphalia was administered by Britain as part of the Allied occupation of Germany. The British unified the former Prussian province of Westphalia (*Westfalen* in German) and the northern part of the Prussian Rhine province (Rheinprovinz) on August 23, 1946. The duchy of Lippe-Detmold was combined with these around six months later, in January 1947.

On June 6, 1950, after three years of discussion, the Landtag of North Rhine-Westphalia by a narrow vote enacted a permanent constitution. This was ratified by the public in a plebiscite of 18 June 1950, with a majority of 57% voting for. This was in accordance with Article 90 of the constitution itself, which demanded such a vote.

Provisions
The constitution, as amended, has 92 articles, covering the operation of the state.

Articles 1, 2 and 3: Fundamental Principles
Article 1 establishes North Rhine-Westphalia as a member state of the Federal Republic of Germany, with its own subdivisions, and its own right to chose a flag and coat of arms (the coat of arms of North Rhine-Westphalia). Article 2 establishes the principle of a plebiscite, and article 3 the separation of powers between parliament and the courts.

Articles 4–29: Fundamental Rights and the Organisation of Community Life

Together, the section covers basic human rights (Article 4), the rights of the family (Articles 5 and 6), education (Articles 7–17), religion and the churches (Articles 18–23), work, the economy and the environment (Articles 24–29).

Articles 30–88: The Bodies and Tasks of the *Land*

This section of the constitution focussed mostly on the operation of the government of North Rhine-Westphalia. The first sub-section cover the actions and organisation of the Landtag (Parliament), with Articles 30–50. Articles 51–64 cover the *Landesregiergung* (State cabinet, similar to the *Bundesregierung*), its interections with the Landtag and some details of the role of the minister-president; articles 65–71 legislation within North Rhine-Westphalia; and articles 72–76 the law courts. Administration is also covered in this section (Articles 77–80), along with financial provisions (Articles 81–88).

Articles 88–92 finished the constitution and its institution, along with the transition to the new system. It is then signed by:

- The Minister-President, Mr Arnold
- The Interior Minister, Dr Menzel
- The Minister for Food, Agriculture and Forestry Mr Lübke
- The Culture Minister, Mr Teusch
- The Finance Minister, Dr Weitz
- The Labour Minister, Mr Halbfell
- The Minister for Reconstruction, Mr Steinhoff
- The Economics Minister, Dr Nölting
- The Social Minister, Dr Amelunxen
- The Justice Minister, Dr Sträter

Source (edited): "http://en.wikipedia.org/wiki/Constitution_of_North_Rhine-Westphalia"